COMMUNITY COLLEGE
READING PROGRAMS

by
Kenneth M. Ahrendt
Oregon State University

Roger Quealy
University of Wisconsin
Reviewing Editor

iRa INTERNATIONAL READING ASSOCIATION
800 Barksdale Road   Newark, Delaware 19711

INTERNATIONAL READING ASSOCIATION

Copyright 1975 by the
International Reading Association

Library of Congress Cataloging in Publication Data

Ahrendt, Kenneth M.
    Community college reading programs.

    Bibliography: p.
    1. Reading (Higher education) I. Title.
LB2395.A35   428'.4'0711   74-31131
ISBN 0-87207-930-9
Second printing, October 1977

CONTENTS

FOREWORD

Do you plan to teach in a community college reading program?

Are you a teacher of reading who suddenly finds himself in a new job in a community college?

Are you a community college instructor over whom your desperate administrator waves his wand and says, "Behold, a reading specialist"?

Are you an administrator toying with the idea of having a wonderful new remedial, corrective, and developmental reading program in a community college but feeling unsure of what it will mean?

Are you a busy person who wants the most needed answers in a very short time?

In any one of these cases, this book is for you. In a single evening you can find out what you want to know. Most of your acquaintances would take much longer to name for you 18 useful standardized tests and describe informal ways to determine a student's reading ability and level; tell you about 79 reading improvement workbooks suitable to the varied abilities, needs, interests, and personalities of community college students; suggest 9 helpful professional organizations from which to learn more information. To be honest, most of your acquaintances probably couldn't begin to do it.

Therefore, I propose that the reader approach this book with a certain amount of gratitude to Kenneth Ahrendt, who must have spoiled many a pleasant hour in your service. Review Editor Roger Quealy also deserves recognition, for he probably would prefer golf, tennis, bridge, or reading, to editing.

Something I treasure about the International Reading Association is that it is full of people who care about what happens to you and your students. If it weren't, I shouldn't have had the pleasure of introducing this book. Now hurry, read it!

Constance M. McCullough, *President*
International Reading Association
1974-1975

PREFACE

The unprecedented growth of the community/junior college in the United States and its open door policy which offers an opportunity to people in all walks of life for a post-secondary education, have created a need for remedial, corrective, and developmental reading programs. These programs are being established at a rate far greater than staff can be trained to teach and administer them. Ten universities are prepared to train community/junior college reading teachers, but little research has been done to determine which is the most viable training program. Insights into this problem, as well as the problem of developing and administering reading programs, are scattered throughout the literature, but heretofore few attempts have been made to consolidate the information for administrators, university personnel, or community/junior college reading teachers. This book is an attempt to provide the information, although it is by no means complete nor is it meant to be a prescription to be followed with painstaking care. The primary purpose is to present what seems to be the best thinking in the field about a variety of topics which concern the teaching of reading at the community/junior college level.

Chapter One describes the college and the unique student body it serves. The purpose is to describe the type of institution the community/junior college has become and the variety of students whose needs it must meet. No attempt has been made to offer a solution to this problem.

The Reading Program as discussed in Chapter Two is a synthesis of the literature available. This synthesis presents the commonalities and some basic principles for the development and operation of a reading program.

Personnel become the heart of any program and Chapter Three presents an analysis and outline for a suggested training program for community/junior college reading teachers. Research in this area is scarce as are training programs for personnel to staff the reading programs.

Diagnosis and Testing is one area which has been sadly neglected and frequently abused, due to lack of professional training of reading personnel. Chapter Four outlines the available instruments for this purpose, and also discusses and illustrates the use of various types of informal diagnostic tools to tie the reading program to the content area subjects and the classroom teacher. While many may not agree with these informal procedures or the standardized test materials discussed, nevertheless we find some guidance and direction from the literature.

There is no one best method for teaching reading improvement at any level nor is there any one best book, machine, or learning system which will fulfill the needs of all community/junior college reading programs. Chapter Five discusses the various materials and hardware available to a reading teacher with cautions and recommendations from the literature. No method of teaching is advocated, but guidelines are offered which cover what we know about learning theory, teaching methods, and student needs.

It is hoped that the material contained in the five chapters and the appendices of this book will serve as a guideline for reading teachers involved in the process of teaching, assist in the planning and development of programs of reading improvement, and provide an explanation and justification for administrators so they may better understand the need for and give one hundred percent support to the reading program in their school.

Roger J. Quealy
Review Editor

the community
college student

Chapter One

THE COMMUNITY COLLEGE STUDENT

THE COLLEGE

Of all the areas of education, the community college has experienced the most rapid growth. More than one community college per week was established during the 1967-1968 academic year. In 1973 there were over 1,000 such institutions. The one distinguishing feature of the community college has been its open-door policy, a policy meaning more than the idea that every student with a high school diploma can enter college. Open-door also means that a student, regardless of level of achievement, ethnic group, or age, will be able to receive the best education possible (7).

The Carnegie Commission affirms that the rapid growth of the community college is due to its open-door policy, geographic distribution in many states, and generally low tuition (11). The community college also offers an opportunity for students who are not fully committed to a four-year college degree to try higher education without great risks of time and money. The community college appeals to the terminal student; the housewife who wants to take classes on a part-time basis; the dropout who wants another chance to obtain marketable job skills; the four-year college student who has failed but wishes to return to the community college to retool; the adult who wants to take special interest courses; the marginal or high-risk student who experienced difficulty finishing high school; the academic transfer who expects to continue his education in a four-year institution; and the minority student who has the opportunity for a low-cost or free post-secondary education. These students compose the student body of the community college; their needs, aspirations, and goals must be dealt with by the college administration and staff.

If its primary purpose is to be a teaching institution, then the community college is ideally suited to cope with the instructional problems of teaching the underachiever, the marginal student, and the academically capable student. Community college research and equipment are teaching-learning oriented; the facilities are generally more committed to teaching than are the facilities of four-year colleges and universities. Many instructional innovations originate at the two-year college (6).

A typical view of a community college shows the academic-transfer, ivy curriculum with departmental or divisional organization on one side of the campus, while on the other side there is the utilitarian, practical program of vocational-technical students and faculty. Furthermore, there is another facet to the community college—the evening college with its smorgasbord of courses and its philosophy of tailoring programs to the interests of students (4).

The traditional role of the two-year college has been its transfer program to the four-year college. Added to this function have been the terminal education programs of vocational-technical training, and now the open-door policy of the community college has further involved the college with the job of salvage, repair, or "rehabilitation" (3).

The community college faces the dilemma of trying to provide a quality education for 1) the academically able student, 2) the high-risk or marginal student, and 3) the vocational or technical student.

THE STUDENT: AN OVERVIEW

The most common characteristic of the community college student which has been studied thoroughly is academic aptitude (12). Several batteries of scholastic aptitude tests—SCAT, STEP, ITBS—have been developed for purposes of admission. One problem which arises when the standard scholastic aptitude tests are used as entrance requirements is that these tests were developed to screen applicants for the four-year college and may not take into consideration the diverse backgrounds and experiences of the community college student. Therefore, validity of these tests for placing students in various programs in the community college is questionable.

The Carnegie Commission points out that community college students are more representative of the college age population of the United States than are students in any other segment of higher education. The Commission also indicates that community college students tend to be almost equally divided between students of above-average and below-average ability (3).

Many studies have found that a majority of the community college freshmen, in all ranges of native ability and prior achievement, express their intentions to transfer to a four-year institution in order to work for a baccalaureate degree. Project Talent found that over one-half of the community college students in the lowest ability quartile wanted to work for a baccalaureate degree (5).

Despite Medsker's findings in his report to the Carnegie Commission, most community college students do not meet the minimum requirements set by the college on the SCAT and are usually placed in remedial programs. Generally speaking, students with academic deficiencies have been placed in developmental or remedial programs which attempt to take the student to a level sufficient for entrance into his desired program of studies (10).

The community college student is usually described in terms of percentiles, stanines, and quartiles. A specific personal description of the student is difficult to compile due to the wide diversity of the population we are attempting to describe and the geographical expanse covered. A description in general terms is necessary, however, because effective and efficient teaching of communication skills in the community/junior college makes it imperative that the reading specialist has formulated in his mind the type of student whom he will teach.

A summarization of the literature indicates that there are certain common characteristics of community/junior college students. As a group they 1) come from families ranging from low to high on the socioeconomic scale; 2) comprise a cross-section of the general population; 3) often are uncertain of their interest and career choices; 4) are more inclined toward vocational education, yet express the desire to transfer to a four-year school; 5) hold part-time jobs and in many instances have been unsuccessful with earlier experiences with traditional approaches to education; 6) represent a wide range of age groups (18-21 and 22 and over, with the median age of 25 years); 7) often need some form of remedial assistance; 8) represent the racial diversity present in the country; and 9) are marginal or high-risk students attracted by the open-door policy. This overview of the community college student is stated in general terms because each school has its own student body and inherent problems.

THE MARGINAL STUDENT

Many community colleges find it necessary to offer remedial education for inadequately prepared students. This need is likely to continue until greater progress is made in overcoming deficiencies of elementary and secondary education in the United States (*11*).

In many community colleges, students are placed in a remedial or developmental program based on their entrance examination scores or on the grade they received in high school. Students who have completed the GED, and who are over 18-years-old, are usually placed in some form of remedial or developmental program. These compensatory programs are designed "to bring the student back" so that he can participate in a program which he has already failed (*10*).

Medsker (*5*) found that, in addition to the high-risk student, the low achiever in high school who "discovers" college quite late and then becomes highly motivated to enroll in a community college transfer program for which he is not equipped, is in need of some type of remedial instruction to fill the gap. Contrary to the opinion of some educational leaders, administrators, and faculty members, many students who enter college lack the language or study skills necessary to insure the probability of success in college level work. The attrition rate of these students is staggering; approximately one of every two students accepted will not remain in college for the period of time necessary to complete the program (*8*).

The rapid growth and open-door policy of the community/junior college introduced the high-risk, marginal student into its student body. Moore (*7*) contends that it is a fair statement that marginal, high-risk students are deficient in the traditional language arts. The failure of the high-risk marginal student to master the basic skills adds frustration to his many past semesters of discontent. This failure also provides teachers with evidence that these students are academically incompetent. Faculty members who have not been trained to meet the needs of the underachiever become discouraged or bored and express their feelings through disinterest or hostility in the guise of advocating normative excellence or selective admissions (6).

The high-risk, marginal student finds himself placed in special programs which are designed (so he is told) to improve his skills and develop his ability to compete with his fellow classmates, and to help him keep up with the reading load placed upon him by faculty members who consider him inferior and a failure at the outset.

SELF-CONCEPT

We are dealing with a student who has a self-concept of failure. Trying to change and improve this self-concept at the post-secondary level is not easy. The student develops the concept of failure through repeated experiences of failure in our educational system.

Our concern is that these students are, in fact, enrolled in some program at the community college and, for the most part, possess inadequate communication skills to function successfully. They cannot read, write, listen, interact, nor communicate on a level which will provide them with the skills necessary to complete a program (1). We must always remember one basic fact of learning: Personal identity or self-concept is a reflection of the reinforcements a student gets from those around him. Many students learn very little because they develop concepts of school and of themselves that are painful. Often, attempts at remediation have been so loaded with familiar punishment and failure associations that successful learning is almost impossible (13).

According to Moore (7), one of the significant discoveries of the marginal, high-risk student occurs as he becomes aware of the opinions of his teachers—the consensus of his instructors is that he cannot learn.

It is important that each learning experience be sufficiently satisfying that the student is stimulated to come back and try again. If the student's learning is to be significant, the act of learning must satisfy one of his needs. The tendency has been to emphasize the work of the teacher, rather than the activity of the student. Teachers must accept the reality of the student's past experiences, even though this is difficult to do. The student cannot escape from the effects of past choices; thus, both he and the teacher must build upon the accumulated past, rather than upon what might have been if different choices had been made.

It is more difficult to diagnose the learning problems of remedial students in the community college than in the elementary or secondary school because the community college student has learned to mask more effectively the symptoms and deficiencies he has in learning. His teachers do not always know where to look for the root of his problems. Frequently, teachers develop the attitude of "Why bother? He doesn't want to learn anyway."

It is true that more than 200 community colleges can identify compensatory or remedial courses being taught; however, it is difficult to locate any college where developmental or remedial departments are integral parts of the total program and where the entire faculty is concerned and involved with the identification and correction of the learning problems of their students (2). The community college must adjust to the students it is serving rather than insisting that the student adjust to the school. Teachers must be ready to teach the culturally distinct student and deal with his different life and linguistic style (9).

MINORITY STUDENTS

Minority students have a rich background of culture which is distinct and different from that of the nonminority student. The minority student also tends to be deficient in language skills, possibly due to his denial of language stimulation through home environment and his bilingual background. In many instances, these factors account for the gross lack of basic skills and motivation seen in other students. The denied student needs special help in acquiring the basic skills necessary to assure successful completion of a program of studies.

The improvement of basic skills should be a part of the total community college curriculum for all students who need this type of assistance. If the open-door policy of the community college is to be a meaningful concept, then this type of integration into the total curriculum is necessary; otherwise, the open-door becomes a revolving door.

References

1. Ahrendt, Kenneth M. "Open or Closed Doors?" *Western College Reading Association Newsletter*, 6 (Fall 1972), 6.
2. Bassone, Jose. "Chicanos in the Community College," *Junior College Journal*, 32 (June/July 1972), 23-26.
3. Carter and Schultz. "The Academic Rehabilitation of Former University Students," *Junior College Journal*, 42 (December), 38.
4. Gleazer, Jr. "Now... To Achieve the Goals," *Junior College Journal*, 42 (May 1972), 20-26.
5. Medsker, Leland L. "The Junior College Student," a report to the Carnegie Corporation, November 1965, 1-30 (mimeo).
6. Meeth, Richard L. "Expanding Faculty Support for Underachievers," *Junior College Journal*, 42 (February 1972), 25-28.
7. Moore, William, Jr. *Against the Odds.* San Francisco: Jossey-Bass, 1970, 4, 11, 169, 222.
8. Peck, Richard E., and Roy Brinkley. "College Reading Services for the Marginal Entrant," *Journal of Reading*, 14 (October 1970), 19.
9. Rouche, John E. *A Modest Proposal: Students Can Learn.* San Francisco: Jossey-Bass, 1972, 17.
10. Sawyer, James M. "Community/Junior Colleges: Tradition in the Future Tense," *Journal of Reading*, 15 (October 1971), 36-40.
11. "The Open Door College: Policies for Community Colleges," a special report and recommendation by the Carnegie Commission on Higher Education, June 1970, 3.
12. Thornton, James W., Jr. *The Community College* (2nd ed.). New York: John Wiley and Sons, 1966, 147.
13. Wilson, Earl. *Psychological Foundations of Learning-Thinking.* New York: McGraw-Hill, 1969, 21, 46-49.

the reading program

Chapter Two

THE READING PROGRAM

According to Anderson (1), when we speak of problems peculiar to the teaching of reading in a community college, we are saying that community college teaching problems in reading are exclusively its own and are not shared with other types of colleges. This statement should be questioned since the four-year school or university which maintains a reading center has students with reading problems similar to those of students at community colleges. Because of its open-door policy, however, the community college does have a concentration of certain types of reading problems not shared in common with other institutions. Because grade point averages and scores received on entrance examinations are still being used for entrance purposes by most four-year colleges and universities, the proportion of marginal and high-risk students allowed to enter is low when compared with the community college.

The uniqueness of reading problems encountered at the community colleges also can be found on many four-year and university campuses operating EOP and Upward Bound programs. Reading problems, however, are unique to the individual student, not to the institution, and must be treated as such. The concern is not how unique the reading problems are to the community college, four-year college, or university per se, but whether the type and scope of program in operation and the development of objectives will meet the individual needs of the institutions.

A review of the literature concerning the various types and scopes of reading programs at the community college level indicates that there are as many varieties of reading improvement programs as there are community colleges and specialists who operate programs. Running throughout the literature, however, is a common thread which indicates that reading improvement programs are usually developed from 1) the specific needs of the institution, 2) the philosophy of the administration, 3) the training of the instructor and his attitude toward reading improvement, and 4) stop-gap measures to facilitate the influx of marginal and high-risk students who have entered the community college due to the open-door policy. Also, many programs originate with a mandate from the faculty and administration to "do something" about the reading and study problems of the student body.

It is difficult to discern programs that are well-planned and involve administration, faculty, and reading staff personnel in their planning. It can be concluded that no one program will fit the needs of any community college. Programs must meet the needs of the individual institution and its student body and should be evaluated, modified, and reviewed as the needs of the students and institution change.

The Eric/Clearinghouse for Community and Junior Colleges published a topical paper, "Community College Reading Center Facilities" by Newman (9), which gives a general overview of the format, facilities, and philosophy used in developing a reading center. Many of the topics discussed provide a foundation for the specialist faced with developing a reading center. Freer (3) identified two major problems in establishing and implementing a college reading program which follows some of the same thinking found in the Eric topical paper. She states, "The lack of motivation and the wide range of abilities in a junior college—from functional illiterates to excellent readers—with standardized reading test scores which range from ten to twenty levels make the establishment and development of a program difficult." She also points out that the lack of good materials to meet this wide range of abilities presents a further problem for the specialist developing a new program.

A more serious problem encountered in the development and operation of a reading center program is the lack of trained, qualified personnel. Moore suggests that instructors in remedial or developmental courses often do not demonstrate any knowledge or understanding of the basic objectives of the course. The instructor often is informed only by the vague objectives which accompany course outlines. Many instructors indicate that their primary objective is to bring the student up to the level of the college credit course.

Kingston (6) provides an overall outline for the development and implementation of a college reading program which, far from being ideal, is a practical approach to the issue. Joffee (4) and Kerstiens (5) support many of Kingston's suggestions and also offer many of the same recommendations. These recommendations and suggestions will be consolidated into an overall format as a framework for the specialist who finds himself faced with the task of having to develop a reading center program.

THE PLANNING OF A PROGRAM

The planning and development of an effective community college reading program must be based upon sound educational and psychological principles, derived from available research evidence. As poor and contradictory as that evidence may be, it is sufficient to provide direction and techniques for the community college program (7). Furthermore, the planner must take into consideration the needs of the students so that a basic philosophy can be formulated upon which a program can be built.

It is important that the administration and total faculty be involved from the first stages of planning. Without this support, a center operates in isolation. Without full understanding of the program, the faculty and the administration may question the need for such an operation.

A good college reading program should provide service to students on all levels of the continuum (6). A careful study of the needs of the students must be made. As mentioned previously, a center cannot operate in isolation. To be successful, a center needs support from counseling units, guidance centers or other student personnel services, and faculty groups and administration (7). All too often the administrator and faculty are not included in planning a center operation. In many instances, the faculty do not realize the purpose of the center or know how they can use its services to their benefit and the benefit of their students. The mere creation of a reading center does not automatically guarantee its acceptance by the students, faculty, and administration.

As Marksheffel (7) states, one of the most important ingredients for planning and directing a reading program is an administration that believes in the need for such a program.

While planning a reading program, it is both prudent and necessary that details of procedure be agreed upon by the instructors and the administration. Once these two groups have reached agreement, a written statement should be prepared which outlines the overall plan and specifies objectives in easily understood terms. The determination of who should be responsible for the reading program is extremely important because it probably will determine the nature of the program and the support it will gain (5).

In summary, the first major step in the development of a good reading program is to involve the administration, faculty, and reading personnel in the planning process to develop the philosophy, objectives, and location of the center.

PHYSICAL FACILITIES

Kerstiens (5) points out that physical facilities play (perhaps unhappily) the most important part in the development of a viable, efficient reading/study skills program. Sometimes facilities dictate the scope of the program, the type of program developed, and the kinds of materials and techniques to be used. Facilities also represent the commitment of the administration to a reading program. Pre-World War II huts, basements, outdated classrooms, and makeshift rooms in remote areas of the campus are some of the types of facilities in use today for reading programs. Many innovative programs are run in the poorest available facilities on campus. On the other hand, many centers are located in carpeted, soundproof centers with elegant furnishings and equipment which make the center attractive.

In the initial planning stages of a program, facilities particularly are a major factor to be considered: How much space is needed? Where should the center be located? What type of lighting, furniture, and fixtures should be used? Early support and commitment by the administration assures interest in the program. Newman (9) describes several centers and furnishings. She cites Portland Community College, Columbia College, and the center at Bakersfield, California, as examples of exemplary centers. The communication type centers at

Lane Community College and Mount Hood Community College offer both tutorial facilities and reading/study skills. These learning centers use the basic philosophy of dealing with the entire communication process for development and improvement rather than isolating one of the communication processes—reading.

Some centers consider study skills to be separate from reading and set up classrooms, areas, or minicourses which concentrate on this difference. This type of facility usually focuses on textbook type reading using SQ3R, ORWET, or other procedures for systematically reading a textbook. Note taking and listening skills are also included in the study skills component.

Unfortunately, the facility in which the program is housed may very well dictate the type of program operated and the commitment of the administration to the program.

SELECTION OF STAFF

It is axiomatic that no program is any better than those who teach it. An inadequately prepared staff can be one of the major weaknesses of an inefficient community college reading program. The staff must have the preparation necessary to work with severely retarded readers, corrective readers, remedial readers, developmental readers, subject matter teachers, and administrators (7).

Staiger (10) states that the teacher can make or break a reading improvement course. The teacher's attitude toward the course is as important as his knowledge. A negative person or a compulsive talker does not belong in a course in which attitudes toward reading and study are being built, and in which silent reading is being practiced. Selection and training of staff is discussed more fully in the following chapter.

THE PROGRAM

The literature is replete with descriptions of various types of reading/study skills programs. The wide range of programs makes it difficult for a person developing a reading program to make an intelligent selection of the best programs to be used as models. An important reason is that each program discussed was designed for a particular school and group of students. Each was based upon the philosophy of that school, its administrative staff, and teaching faculty. Essentially, all programs contain certain elements which are basic to the development of a reading/study skills program.

THE CENTER

The center is the facility for developing, practicing, applying, and (eventually) enjoying reading and learning. It is a facility for individual, small group, and large group learning; for discussions; teacher conferences; tutoring; testing; and counseling (2). It is the heart of the reading program. The physical make-up of the center depends upon several factors: Was the center built as part of the total building plan of the college? Is the center a remodeled classroom or area that was used for some other purpose? Is the center part of the library or a self-learning complex? Is the center an outdated bungalow or building which has been remodeled to make do? Are the furniture and fixtures new, comfortable, adaptable for group and individual work sessions? Are carrels part of the center complex? Does the center have multipurpose rooms?

Surveys indicate that the ideal center is a multipurpose communication or learning complex with facilities for arrangements which can accommodate any learning situation the staff wants to create. Attached to, or part of, the center are faculty offices and workrooms so the students have immediate access to instructors for conferences and counseling.

TYPE OF PROGRAM

A well-developed and planned reading/study skills program will have as its objective the needs of the student body of the college it serves. The program will teach communication skills to developmental, remedial, corrective, and clinical readers. The teaching of reading at the college level has three specific functions—to stimulate, inform, and guide students. In this sequence, the emphasis should be placed upon stimulation and guidance rather than upon the process of providing information about reading which the student may feel is quite unrelated to his work in college. In general, students do not hunger and thirst for information concerning how to read until they understand that the reading skills are directly related to their success in college. Remedial students, like other students, are motivated when they like what they are doing. The academically slow student looks for relevance in that which he is expected to learn. The improvement of basic skills is the prerequisite to most learning in the formal classroom. Mastery of these skills will open the door to many intellectual, vocational, and economic alternatives. Without these skills, few opportunities are available (*8*).

Tremonti (*11*) summarized the types of programs and their components which operate in the community college:

> There are four parts to any reading program in a school. The first part consists of the regular developmental reading program which teaches basic reading skills of word recognition and comprehension. The second part is the remedial program which is necessary for the student who simply did not achieve to his capacity in the developmental program or missed it entirely, and it is necessary and essential to have this work. The third part is the application of these skills in all content subjects, whether they be math, English, history or literature by the subject area teachers in the community college. The fourth part of the reading program is supplementary reading that is provided for through access to an extensive number of textbooks as additional reading to basic studies as well as a varied supply of library books that are used in connection with the content subject as background and as unrestricted free reading.

THE REMEDIAL PROGRAM

The majority of community colleges operate some type of remedial program for students who score in the lower 25th quartile on the entrance examination or on a standardized reading test and whose reading inadequacies impede their learning. Remedial programs require a trained specialist, a wide variety of materials, and a low student-teacher ratio. Teaching is centered upon student basic skill deficiencies, such as word attack and comprehension skills. The materials used are usually considered to be high-interest, low-readability. The underlying philosophy in a remedial program is to afford the student large doses of success to change his self-concept from one of failure to one of success.

Regardless of the techniques used in the instruction of reading in the remedial program, much of the content deals with subjects such as adventure, sports, patriotism, and morality. These subjects may interest the young adult remedial reader. Much of the material in remedial reading classes is considered trivia by the high-risk student because the information does not offer him a readily seen direct relationship to his life and the world. In fact, some materials may even contradict much of what the student experiences in the real world (2). Many remedial programs use materials which are written for elementary and secondary students and do not hold the interest of the high-risk, marginal, or remedial student.

Instruction should be simple, direct, and specific. It should emphasize reading as a thinking skill and as a purposeful process of identifying, interpreting, and evaluating ideas. Instruction should be concerned with practical procedures rather than with abstract theory about reading. It should consist of well-structured directions to the student as to how various reading skills can be developed and applied to subject matter areas where he has the greatest concern and where he needs help to pass a course, regardless of how poor his skill development may be (2).

THE DEVELOPMENTAL PROGRAM

The developmental program is viewed by most reading specialists as a class offered for credit or no credit. The academically capable student is given group instruction in a wide range of reading skills, usually through the lecture method. Various skills such as vocabulary building, improvement of rate and comprehension, and skimming and scanning are discussed by the instructor and then the student is given the opportunity to practice these skills using commercially prepared materials. *Vocabulary for College* or *How to Improve Your Vocabulary* offer student exercises in vocabulary building. Exercises for comprehension improvement are provided in Brown's *Efficient Reading*, Strang's *Study Type Exercises for College*, and Judson's *Techniques of Reading*. Skimming and scanning practice is offered in Maxwell's *Skimming and Scanning Exercises*, Spache and Berg's *The Art of Efficient Reading* (2nd ed.), and others. In this type of class situation, transfer is not automatic because of the exposure to skill development; it must be taught. Practice in the trade material provides a beginning, but the skills taught must be transferred to the text the student uses to make the practice meaningful and useful to him; otherwise, the developmental course has served no practical purpose. Each student should know how well he reads and should select for himself the specific reading skills he needs to acquire. The student should understand that he can improve his own reading ability and that he must assume the responsibility for doing so. Many students have experienced academic failure and are inadequately prepared to handle the lecture-practice activity of a developmental reading course. The need is to improve self-concepts and modify attitudes toward self and school. Attitudes can be changed so that the student recognizes that he is the master of his own choices. He needs tangible proof that he can and is improving. Instructors can show by actions and words that they have confidence in the effectiveness of the materials they are presenting and that they are aware of the effort a student is putting forth to become a better reader.

THE CONTENT AREA TEACHER AND READING

The subject matter teacher is the one person who can give the most help and assistance in aiding students to develop their reading skills in the content area. He is the expert in his field who knows the vocabulary which must be learned and can set the appropriate purposes for reading.

The reading improvement instructor must establish rapport with content area teachers to help them identify the various methods through which they can help students become better readers.

There are several ways in which the reading specialist can assist content area teachers. One way is to help determine the readability levels of the textbooks. Many content teachers are not aware of the concept of readability or how a textbook can be written at a level too difficult for a student, thus causing reading and learning problems. Second, the reading specialist can help the content teacher construct group informal inventories to be administered to students to determine reading ability. These inventories can be used to identify students who are reading at the independent, instructional, and frustrational levels. The specialist can show the teacher how to group his class according to the results of the group informal inventory and can suggest various types of materials which can be used to meet student needs. Third, the specialist can assist further by giving demonstration-directed teaching lessons which show the content teacher how to introduce new vocabulary, set purposes for reading, discuss and point out new concepts students will meet in reading, and change paragraph headings into questions to be read and answered by students. The specialist also can demonstrate how to structure the oral discussion period using literal, interpretative, and vocabulary questions to check student comprehension of the material read. Furthermore, the specialist can make available lists of supplementary content area books, written at various levels of readability, to be used with students who cannot read the textbook or who need independent instruction and can profit from independent work.

The specialist can assist the instructor in the use of the communication or learning center. Basically, the role of the specialist becomes one of a resource person who helps the content teacher in the ways discussed to make the learning experience more meaningful for students.

Without cooperation between the content area teacher and the specialist, the reading program in any community college operates in isolation and does not afford the type of transfer of learning that will benefit the student and make the development of reading skills meaningful.

THE LEARNING/COMMUNICATION CENTER COMPLEX

The concept of the learning/communication center complex is somewhat new to reading in the community college. The name implies something more than a facility for teaching reading/study skills; it embraces the concepts of self-learning, learning assistance on an individual basis, tutorial assistance, and involvement of content area instructors. Lane Community College is an example of a learning/communication center. The center staff consists of twenty people—three full-time reading instructors, two half-time math instructors, one part-time business instructor, and one half-time English instructor as a second language specialist. Paraprofessionals are used to assist instructors and students in the center (2). It can be seen that with types of differential staffing, a center becomes not just a place to practice reading/study skills, but a complete learning facility where the student can get help with his learning problem. Self-instructional materials in content areas, such as math, English, science, and history, are available for student use in such a center. The uniqueness of such a center is that the whole communication/learning process of the student is treated. Reading/study skills are placed in proper perspective as part of the total communication process. This type of center affords the student an opportunity to see the relationship between learning and the communication process and how they fit together to assist him in becoming an independent learner. Learning becomes the responsibility of the student. He sees the need for and the relevance of such learning and is motivated to succeed and progress at his own rate. In this type of center, the faculty has the opportunity to place materials for independent student use and to volunteer tutor service in the various content areas when needed.

The learning/communication center concept allows for the involvement of the entire community college faculty and student body in assisting students to become independent learners and affords services which usually are not available in reading/study skills centers.

THE READING PROGRAM
AND THE COMMUNITY COLLEGE

The purpose of a well-planned community college reading program is to be of service to the entire college student body and staff. It should never be intended only to be a service which provides remedial assistance to a small segment of the college population.

A reading program must justify its existence as an integral part of the total college program by: 1) offering consulting services to the institution in the various ways mentioned; 2) providing a developmental program for the entire student body, incorporating the elements of study skills, comprehension development, rate, and research usage; and 3) including a service for the remedial student who needs specialized assistance and guidance with his reading skills.

The staff of the center must serve as a resource to the entire college faculty; the college faculty and administration will become involved in the operation of the center only if they understand its purpose and role in the community college.

References

1. Anderson, Clarence. "Problems of Individualization," *Reading: The Right to Participate*, Twentieth Yearbook National Reading Conference, 1971, 221-224.

2. Carter and McGinnis. "Some Factors to Be Considered in Conducting a College-Adult Reading Program," *Junior College and Adult Reading Programs: Expanding Fields*, Sixteenth Yearbook National Reading Conference, 1967, 68-73.

3. Freer, Imagene. "Problems of Junior College Reading Programs," *Reading: The Right to Participate*, Twentieth Yearbook National Reading Conference, 1971, 206-210.

4. Joffee, Irwin. "The All School Reading Program at the Junior College Level," Proceedings of the First Annual Conference of WCRA, 1968, 28-33.

5. Kerstiens, Gene. "College Reading: Where is It?" *Reading: Putting all the Cards on the Table*, Fourth Annual Proceedings of WCRA, 1972, 9, 75-80.

6. Kingston, Albert J., Jr. "Problems of Initiating a New College Reading Program," *Starting and Improving College Reading Programs*, Eighth Yearbook National Reading Conference, 1959, 15-24.

7. Marksheffel, Ned D. "Planning a Junior College Reading Program," *Junior College Reading Programs*. Newark, Delaware: International Reading Association, 1967, 8-13.

8. Moore, William, Jr. *Against the Odds*. San Francisco: Jossey-Bass, 1970, 10, 171-172-196.

9. Newman, Loretta. "Community College Reading Facilities," *Eric/ Clearinghouse for Junior Colleges*, Topical Paper No. 21, 1971, 1-9.

10. Staiger, Ralph C. "Initiating the College or Adult Reading Program," *Research and Evaluation in College Reading*, Ninth Yearbook National Reading Conference, 1960, 121.

11. Tremonti, Joseph B. "Improving the Junior College Reading Program," *The Psychology of Reading Behavior*, Eighteenth Yearbook National Reading Conference, 1969, 246-252.

teaching personnel

Chapter Three

TEACHING PERSONNEL

One of the most important responsibilities of the community college is to provide its students with a developmental and, if necessary, remedial education, especially in reading and study skills. The open-door policy of the community college has made this responsibility a mandate. It admits students who are marginal, low-achievers, lacking in the necessary communication skills to succeed in any program in which they may choose to enroll. Bossone (3) found that programs were failing to meet the needs of the students enrolled, and the major factor for this failure was inadequate and/or unenthusiastic teachers. Rouche (10) found similar failure of programs for basically the same reason—inadequately trained staff.

Moore (7) states that teachers of remedial students at the college level are, for the most part, self-trained. They have operated on a learn-as-you-go or on-the-job training basis and their jobs have been without description, structure, theory, or methodology. Many of the teachers assigned to remedial classes have neither the desire nor the temperament to work with remedial students.

In "Training Faculty for Junior College Reading Programs," Kazmierski (4) concludes that comprehensive studies of the professional background and experience of current junior college reading and study skills instructors have been limited. The data must be gathered from several surveys conducted on the training of junior college reading instructors. These surveys indicate that, at present, a master's degree is the basic acceptable preparation for junior college instructors. Preparation for the masters is not even in college reading, let alone a reading specialty. Many instructors of reading at the community college are assigned from various departments, such as English and psychology, and have no formal preparation for teaching the reading/study skills course. There have also been situations in which persons outside the teaching profession have been hired to teach reading courses (9). In 1972, Kerstiens (5) expressed concern that the training and preparation of community college reading and study skills instructors had not changed noticeably since Maxwell's survey in 1967.

Colleges and universities have been slow to develop training programs for the person wishing to enter the field of reading at the community college level. Most programs in existence are based on training elementary and secondary reading teachers and remedial specialists. Therefore, a person who wishes to specialize in community college reading must train in these programs and then retool on the job. There is a severe lack of trained, competent reading personnel available for the community college.

Several programs have been developed for training community college teachers. How many of these programs have been put into the curriculum of institutions of higher learning is impossible to determine because of the lack of available research on the topic.

TRAINING PROGRAMS

Kazmierski (4), Maxwell (6), and Price and Wolf (9), have outlined training programs for teachers of reading at the college level. These programs have many elements in common. Price and Wolf have written an extensive program for training reading instructors. They advocate that even though there is a critical shortage of trained reading personnel, this should be no reason for weakening any program or taking short cuts to fill positions available in the field.

The most important step to be taken in training community/junior college personnel is the process of selection of the candidates to be admitted to such a program. Using Price and Wolf's criteria there are four personal qualities which must be considered in the selection of a reading teacher. The candidate must: 1) display personal attributes which contribute to the making of a "good teacher"; 2) have a genuine regard for students; 3) be flexible and creative; and 4) possess qualities of leadership and the ability to work with people (9).

This set of criteria seems severe, but we must consider that in many community colleges there are only one or two reading teachers who must work with the administration and faculty and administer the program at the same time.

Kazmierski (4) points out that the community college reading instructor must plan for the variances in course structure, individual instructional needs, and selection of instructional media. Perhaps even more crucial is understanding the immense differences in psychological makeup and motivation due to the mixed population of the community college.

The American Association of Junior Colleges has taken a strong position on the training of personnel. They have set general guidelines to be followed by universities in their programs for preparing junior college personnel. Unfortunately, the only guidelines available for the training of reading personnel are those found in the International Reading Association's "Roles, Responsibilities, and Qualifications of Reading Specialists," and the specific suggestions of Price, Wolf, and Kazmierski.

In addition to personal qualifications, consideration must be given to the academic preparation of the college reading instructor. The education of the junior college reading instructor can be divided into three parts: general education, specialized training, and the community college curriculum and history. Together, the three components make for a highly specialized reading instructor, adequately prepared to teach in a community college reading program.

General Education

Price and Wolf (9) suggest that the curriculum for the college reading instructor should include literature, social studies, sciences, and the arts. As part of his general preparation, the teacher should be well informed and have an abiding interest in current events. This is a broad education. Such a curriculum acquaints the student teacher with the areas of knowledge needed to teach reading in the content areas at the community college level. No one advocates that the teacher become a specialist in all of these areas but that he have some preparation in them above the high school level.

Specialized Education

The college reading teacher must have intensive specialized preparation in the understanding of the reading process and all of its components. It is recommended that he have course work in 1) diagnostic techniques, 2) principles and practices of remediation, 3) methods of teaching reading and study skills, 4) methods of teaching reading in the content areas of the junior college, 5) program development and supervision, 6) psychological testing, 7) communication skills, 8) evaluation or research, and 9) practicum in the field.

These courses can be grouped for purposes of discussion into 1) diagnosis and remediation, 2) materials and methods, 3) course development and supervision, and 4) field experience.

Diagnosis and remediation. It is necessary that a college reading instructor be able to diagnose and establish a course of remediation for students and he should have a thorough knowledge of the standardized tests available for college level administration, what they measure, and how to interpret results. He should also be acquainted with informal testing techniques (group and individual informal inventories, word recognition inventories, skills inventories) and be able to interpret and use the results to plan a program of remediation for students.

Remediation is the carrying out of a plan of instruction to correct a student's reading difficulties. This requires the college reading instructor to plan the program which best meets the student's individual needs. As Triggs (*11*) states, the main objective of any college remedial program should be to give a student proficiency in the reading skills he needs to do his college work satisfactorily. The program may also aim to broaden the student's use of reading to meet the responsibilities and problems he faces in college and afterwards. The second possible objective of remedial reading—to encourage students to read more widely and more intelligently—is education in general. Triggs speculates that how far the remedial program contributes to the objectives stated can be determined only subjectively by the teacher as he watches the student's reading habits change and grow.

Materials and methods. A wide variety of materials now available for the prospective college reading teacher includes college reading improvement materials, media, hardware, and content materials used in the community college. As Price and Wolf (15) point out, teachers should be able to use specific reading materials (including commercially prepared aids, textbooks, and workbooks) and should have a knowledge of mechanical devices in order to make a critical judgment as to the merit and purpose of a particular machine. An area not to be overlooked is that of teacher-prepared materials. The need arises to learn how to design materials for specific purposes because of the diverse backgrounds and abilities of the students found in the typical open-door community college.

Course development and supervision. Many a college reading teacher has had to develop a program from scratch. His basic equipment may consist of a room, some furniture, a request for renovation, and a budget from the administration. He must be able to set down a program philosophy, objectives, and means of student selection and evaluation. Furthermore, he must order supplies, equipment, program materials, hardware, and workbooks. It is necessary that the teacher have some training in how to write broad and specific program objectives, as well as student objectives and goals, in order to operate an effective program.

Supervision experience is of the utmost importance because the reading teacher will be dealing with other faculty members, tutors, and, in some instances, paraprofessionals and support personnel. The teacher must have the ability to supervise this personnel wisely and with understanding and yet develop the most efficient working team possible to run an effective program.

Field experience. The most important element of a training program for a prospective college reading teacher is the practicum or field experience. The practicum affords the student the opportunity to work in a reading center under the supervision of an experienced reading instructor. The field experience allows the prospective teacher to observe teaching techniques, examine materials, ask questions, and begin to participate in classroom activities.

The practicum experience should include lesson preparation, teacher-made materials, small group skills lessons, and tutoring, as well as teaching the class reading and study skills.

At all times during the practicum experience there should be an opportunity for the prospective teacher to have conferences or engage in seminars with the regular teaching staff. He should be closely supervised at first and gradually released to teach on his own. The value of the practicum allows the prospective teacher to practice the theory he has learned and associate and deal with students in a reading center situation. He should not be used as a clerk or as supplementary staff personnel but should be allowed to participate in the center as part of the learning experience. Through the practicum experience, the prospective teacher will gain insights and experiences in dealing with the wide range and variety of reading achievement levels found in a community college reading center.

Community College Curriculum and History

It is important for the prospective teacher to understand the history and development of the community college and its curriculum. A knowledge of the curriculum of the community college will give the prospective teacher an insight into the various content areas of the college and will allow him to develop his program according to the needs of the students and faculty. Furthermore, an understanding of the curriculum allows for the planning of skills exercises in the content areas. The prospective reading teacher can work closely with the content area teacher by helping him run readability formulae on the textbooks he chooses for his classes, develop informal reading inventories, and give demonstrations in using the directed teaching activity. He is also in a better position to explain to the faculty and administration the relationship between the college curriculum and the learning or reading center.

A knowledge and understanding of the background development of the community/junior college gives the reading teacher a perspective of this segment of education and allows him to structure a framework of reference in which to work. The prospective teacher should acquire an understanding of the community/junior college, how the open-door policy developed, the problems of such an institution, and the diversity of the faculty and student body.

PARAPROFESSIONALS AND TUTORS

Frustration is the key word when a search is made to hire a reading specialist to teach in a college reading program. Many program directors have found it necessary to train their own instructors or train paraprofessionals to assist in the operation of the reading program.

When the decision is made to use and train a person as a paraprofessional, the role the person will serve in the reading program will be defined through questions such as: Should the person selected have a bachelor's degree or at least some college training? Should only graduate students in reading be considered? Should the person under consideration have any training in reading education and, if so, at what level? What role will the paraprofessional play in the reading program? All of these questions and many more need to be considered and explored before the selection process or training program begins.

In choosing personnel for the program, consideration must be given to the basic philosophy of the reading program and the instructors involved. The training and use of the paraprofessional in a reading center must be accepted by the entire staff and the administration. Many times in the field of reading we hesitate to use unskilled or untrained people because we expect instructors to be specialists. Even so, the specialist needs some help if he is to help students to function successfully. The alternative of training a person to give help has proven to be both practical and successful. It is a matter of priorities as to what can be done to relieve the instructor to help each student reach his full reading potential.

Training sequence. Ahrendt (2) devised a training program for paraprofessionals. It was believed that one of the best ways to begin the training process was for the personnel selected to take the reading improvement course. It is difficult, though not impossible, to teach something you do not know yourself. Therefore, being enrolled in and taking the reading improvement course exposes the trainee to both sides of the coin: as a student in a learning situation and as an observer of the teaching methods used in the program.

After the completion of the reading improvement course, each trainee was placed under the supervision of an experienced instructor—somewhat similar to a student teaching experience. He was then given the responsibility, under supervision, of teaching certain areas of the program. For example, the trainee might be asked to prepare a session on previewing or textbook reading. The material was prepared by the trainee, checked by the instructor, discussed by them both for possible deletions or additions; then the trainee presented the lesson in class. This method permits the selection of the best candidates to become paraprofessionals in the reading center.

In order to develop the training sequence and select paraprofessionals to work in the program, a reasonable set of criteria had to be established. Because the trainee had no background in reading other than the reading improvement course itself, a basic foundation in reading had to be built.

Trainees were required to complete readings in materials describing reading skill development. Prereading questions were developed to give the candidate direction and purpose for his reading activity and to enable him to answer questions posed by the instructor. Each trainee received instruction on the use and abuse of the reading accelerator, the controlled reader, and the skimmer and scanner and was required to read carefully the instructor's manuals for each instrument.

The paraprofessional was also trained in the administration and scoring of standardized tests used in the program. Test interpretations were done by the instructor. The paraprofessional was trained as well in teaching study skills. Many paraprofessionals selected were not education majors, but they did have other academic or technical training. This background proved to be valuable to students in the reading improvement program because the paraprofessional could help students in basic study skills in his own area of concentration. Since no one study technique was advocated to the exclusion of others, the paraprofessional examined and learned all the techniques and then synthesized one technique which would work best in his particular area. The paraprofessional also was trained to supervise the laboratory sessions, for a person is needed in an open center at all times to supervise and give assistance to students.

To familiarize the paraprofessional with the wide range of materials and workbooks available in the field of college reading, specific bibliographies were developed, based on skill development or academic subject areas. Each piece of material was examined and the readings contained in the material were classified under the proper topic. The paraprofessional was responsible for checking student work, giving further directions, and reporting the results to the instructor. Periodic meetings or seminars were held with the paraprofessionals and instructors to discuss problems that may have arisen and to develop teacher-made materials to assist students.

TUTORS

Adams (*1*) and Newman (*8*) developed programs for the use of tutors in a community college reading laboratory. The training procedures and selection process for tutors in these programs were basically the same. Important requirements in the selection of tutors (expressed in both training programs) were that tutors should: 1) genuinely like and want to help people, 2) be able to demonstrate their ability to be at ease with others, and 3) have a capacity to communicate with students.

All tutors were required to meet with the program instructors at least once a week. They were also assigned readings that would give them some background and insight into the reading process. Adams required tutors to function in the following capacities:

1. Clarify objectives and show the tutee how to use various lab materials and equipment.
2. Give the student encouragement and confidence.
3. Encourage attendance and follow up on student absences by calling or sending notes to his home.
4. Review with the student his corrected papers and lab work to make certain he understands all mistakes indicated.
5. Keep the section instructor informed of the student's progress.
6. Listen to the student's complaints or problems.
7. Encourage the student to keep his file folder up-to-date.

Tutors were required to meet frequently with instructors to keep abreast of new course objectives and materials and also to receive further training and assistance in their work.

Newman states that the duties of tutors are to check homework, attend conferences, manage conferences, keep anecdotal records of tutees should anything unusual occur, and discuss problems with the instructor. Tutors further are trained to score pre- and posttests, work in the lab, teach small groups in various skill areas, and assist the instructor.

Yuthas (*12*) conducted an experiment using tutors in a college reading improvement class. The tutors were trained by the instructors to use SRA Laboratory 111b, SRA's *Reading for Understanding* (general edition), and the GH filmstrips from EDL with the controlled reader. Tutors led discussions about study skills and notetaking. Yuthas' findings indicated that those classes who had tutors working with instructors made greater gains and had a lower dropout rate than classes taught by instructors only.

In order to free the instructor to give more individual attention to students, it is necessary to employ the assistance of either paraprofessionals or tutors or both. Kerstiens (*5*) sums up the valuable assistance provided by the paraprofessional and tutor:

> Since the paraprofessionals are usually younger people, they answer a need for energetic and empathetic technicians and tutors to sustain clients' learning activities in the laboratory; consequently, they prove invaluable to the practitioner who attempts to effect individualized learning.

The professional equipped with a support team trained to assist him in the process of instruction can truly begin to individualize the learning process in the reading center and assist more students on an individual basis.

References
1. Adams, Royce W. "The Use of Tutors in Santa Barbara City College Reading Laboratory," 3-7.
2. Ahrendt, Kenneth M. "Paraprofessionals in the College Reading Program," Fourth Annual Proceedings WCRA, 1971, 8-14.
3. Bossone, Richard M. *Remedial English Instruction in California Public Junior Colleges: An Analysis and Evaluation of Current Practices.* Sacramento: California State Department of Education, September 1969.

4. Kazmierski, Paul R. "Training Faculty for Junior College Reading Programs," *Eric/Clearinghouse for Junior Colleges*, Topical Paper No. 24, May 1971, 2-4.

5. Kerstiens, Gene. "College Reading: Where Is It?" *Reading: Putting All the Cards on the Table*, Fifth Annual Proceedings WCRA, 1972, 75-83.

6. Maxwell, Martha. "What the College Reading Teacher Needs to Know About Reading," Second Annual Proceedings WCRA, 1969, 65-70.

7. Moore, William, Jr. *Against the Odds*. San Francisco: Jossey-Bass, 1970, 70.

8. Newman, Loretta. "The Paraprofessional in the Community College Reading and Study Center," *Eric/Clearinghouse for Junior Colleges*, Topical Paper, 99-106.

9. Price, Umberto, and Kay Wolfe. "Teacher Preparation of the Junior College Reading Teacher," *Junior College Reading Programs*. Newark, Delaware: International Reading Association, 1967, 1-7.

10. Rouche, John E. "Salvage, Redirection, or Custody? Remedial Education in the Community Colleges," *Eric/American Association of Junior Colleges*, Monograph No. 1, 1968.

11. Triggs, Frances. *Remedial Reading: The Diagnosis and Correction of Reading Difficulties at the College Level*, 1948, 8-9.

12. Yuthas, Ladessa. "Student Tutors in a College Remedial Program," *Journal of Reading*, 14 (January 1971), 231-234.

diagnosis and testing

Chapter Four

DIAGNOSIS AND TESTING

The teaching of reading, if it is to be effective, should be based on a thorough knowledge of the reading strengths and weaknesses of students (3). Typically, some form of standardized testing is used to obtain this information. However, to obtain an accurate assessment of student achievement, it is advisable to use a wide variety of reading measures including informal inventories, standardized tests, teacher observations, and teacher assessment of a student's performance in the content areas.

One of the major problems faced by the community college reading specialist is the lack of a wide variety of standardized survey or diagnostic tests. Goodwin (4) found that 60 percent of the 300 reading teachers he surveyed considered as diagnostic the standardized test given to community/junior college reading students at the beginning of the course. This practice was followed despite the fact that three tests often selected for use (Nelson-Denny Reading Test, Iowa Silent Reading Test, and Cooperative Reading Test) were survey tests (2). Evans and Dubois' evaluation of these tests shows that the tests yield only grade level or percentile scores in general comprehension and vocabulary, and tell little more than whether a particular student can read at a certain level or whether his vocabulary is adequate. The tests tell nothing about the student's particular reading deficiencies—the most important considerations in a remedial or developmental reading course. At best, these tests can be called screening devices; and further testing must be done to determine specific reading deficiencies. The tests also compare students in terms of general reading achievement.

A current reading test, developed by Raygor as part of the McGraw-Hill Basic Skills System, measures rate, recall of facts, skimming and scanning, and paragraph comprehension. The student reads two selections—an easy passage and a passage from a textbook. He reads for three minutes, stops, marks the line on which he stopped when the time elapsed, and then continues reading for another two minutes. He then answers ten comprehension questions (which follow each reading selection) to test recall of what he has read.

The second section of the test is devoted to skimming and scanning from a variety of textbook materials, tables of contents, and indexes.

The third part of the test is called paragraph comprehension. There are 30 items in this section of the test and each question is classified as it relates to one of six general areas of reading comprehension: the ability to recognize main ideas, specific facts, scientific principles, paragraph organization, author intent, and author tone. Five questions are geared to each of the subskills in this portion of the test. Even though five may not be a sufficient number of questions upon which to judge a student's performance, this test is helpful because it is more diagnostic in nature than any of the other reading tests available for the community/junior college population. Also, the test is normed on the two-year school population. No grade level designation is given—only raw score, standard score, percentile rank, and stanine. The inherent value is that this test can be used as a teaching device if the reading teacher goes over the test scores with students and identifies specific areas of weakness and strength. Although this instrument is new, and not widely used, it affords a broader scope of insight into some specific areas of reading deficiencies for a special population—the community/junior college student.

A widely used reading test is the Nelson-Denny Reading Test for High School and College (Forms A,B,C,D). This test has two advantages: it can be administered in a relatively short period of time (forty minutes) and it has two types of answer sheets (self-marking and machine scoring). The self-marking answer sheet is most commonly used because as the student marks on the answer sheet his answers are reproduced on the response pad by means of a carbon insert. Either the instructor or the student can separate the answer sheet, count the number of correct responses, and transfer the following test information to the block form on the front of the sheet: raw scores and percentiles for vocabulary, comprehension, total score, and rate score of the test. The Nelson-Denny provides grade level scores, as well as norms for adults, and when the test is used for these purposes, administration time is reduced.

Another test frequently used by reading centers is the Diagnostic Reading Test, more commonly known as the Triggs Test. The range of this test extends from grade seven through college freshman. Both the Survey and the Diagnostic sections come in three forms, A, B, and C.

The Survey Section of the Diagnostic Reading test battery may be used as an independent test or as a screening device to show to whom the total battery or selected portions should be administered. The Survey Section has three subtests: general reading, vocabulary, and comprehension. The Diagnostic Reading Test measures reading performance in these major areas: vocabulary, comprehension (silent and auditory); rates of reading in science and social studies materials and flexibility of reading rate according to purpose on general nature material; and word recognition (3).

Most reading programs use some form of evaluation of study skills. The Brown and Holtzman Survey of Study Habits and Attitudes is one test used; and the 1965 edition is available in one form—C. Machine scored as well as hand scored answer sheets are available. Hand scoring of the test is a long, tedious process, as there are six separate answer keys which must be used. A counseling key and a diagnostic key are provided. The counseling key enables the reading specialist and the student to identify and discuss items missed on the test. The diagnostic key or profile provides the user with a convenient method of summarizing the SHHA results graphically on the back of the answer sheet. The test reports raw scores and percentile ranks.

The Study Habits score is found by totalling the Delay Avoidance and Work Methods scores; the Study Attitudes score is found by totalling the Teacher Approval and Education Acceptance scores; and the Study Orientation score is obtained by totalling the Study Habits and Study Attitudes scores.

The California Study Methods Survey ranges from grades 7 to 13. It is a self-reporting inventory designed to reveal the essential nature of the study methods and attitudes of the student. The CSMS is made up of 150 standardized questions which reflect the consistent differences in study methods and attitudes between high achieving and low achieving students. The Survey is keyed to yield the following scores: 1) attitude toward school, 2) mechanics of study, 3) planning and system, and 4) verification (*1*). The test has only one form.

The Study Skills test of the McGraw-Hill Basic Skills System offers information not found in the above mentioned tests; it measures the student's skills in problem solving, underlining, library information, and study skills information. It also includes an attitude survey toward study skills.

Due to the recency of its appearance, little research is available on Basic Skills System's Reading and Study Skills Test. Furthermore, some reading teachers are reluctant to change from a favorite test to a new test because they are not familiar enough with educational measurements and argue that the Basic Skills Tests take too long to administer.

In summary, the standardized reading tests are quite limited in what they measure and diagnose. There are few tests on the market which measure reading achievement in specific subjects.

INFORMAL INVENTORIES

Other vehicles which can be used to diagnose reading deficiencies are individual and group informal inventories. The use and development of the group informal inventory can measure a student's achievement and difficulties in the content areas. It is important for the content area teacher and the reading specialist to have this information because, regardless of the reading deficiencies any student may have, it is necessary for a student to function successfully in the content areas. He must pass content courses in order to complete his program of studies. Despite the concept of individualization and group teaching which has been advocated by reading specialists and classroom teachers, little individual work actually is done in the classroom. Programed and self-instructional materials must be read with success. To determine the amount of success a student will have in any content area and the mode or method used to teach the content, it is necessary to determine the reading level of the student in the content classroom and in the study skills center. Both the specialist and content teacher need this information to effect viable and productive achievement on the part of the student.

To determine reading levels and skill weaknesses, Eller (*1*) has suggested a college level procedure for using informal tests which includes samples from the texts used in basic freshmen science, social studies, and English courses. Eller further recommends that this informal approach be used by the reading teacher or the subject matter teacher to diagnose other skills, ". . . he can easily begin to 'specialize' in the development of special collections of exercises for the appraisal of note-taking skills, evaluation skills, abilities concerned with the organization of information, and vocational and reference skills."

According to Farr (*3*) the feature most often overlooked in the use of informal inventories is their use as a daily, continuous part of reading instruction. By constantly being alert to each student's reading performance, the teacher can adjust the instructional materials to insure continued success.

A reading or learning center should have a file of informal group inventories in each of the content subjects normally taken by freshmen and sophomore students. The administration of these tests can give the reading specialist a diagnostic picture of a student's specific areas of weakness in content subjects.

Construction of group informal inventories is a fairly simple process. However, readability of the passages must be taken into consideration when constructing the inventory. There are many readability formulae a teacher can use from the most complex (Dale-Chall), to the simplest (Fry Readability Graph or the Flesch Formula). Which formula you use depends upon how accurate you choose to be and the time you have available.

Passages used in an informal inventory should be taken from the textbook the student will use for instruction. These reading materials help establish the student's instructional reading level—the level at which he can read independently with some teacher assistance without using material which is so difficult that it frustrates and defeats him. The student should be able to understand 70 percent of the material read without teacher help. The passages selected should not be taken from the beginning of the text as they tend to be fairly simple and not representative of the book. Choose a passage of approximately 500-600 words in length from the middle third or last section of the text. Be sure that it is not necessary for the student to refer to charts, maps, graphs, or other visual aids. Apply a readability formula to determine the approximate grade level of the passage; then construct questions for the selection. The questions should follow the sequence of the material as the author presents it rather than in random fashion. To eliminate the element of guess, Marksheffel (6), and Johnson and Kress (5), recommend that the questions be open-ended rather than multiple-choice, true-false, or yes-no questions.

There should be a minimum of ten questions developed for a passage and they should be of three types: fact, vocabulary, and inference. Fact questions test the student's knowledge of facts found in the reading; vocabulary understanding and inference can be deduced by making use of factual knowledge gained from the selection.

Marksheffel suggests that it is better to ask vocabulary, fact, and inference type questions as they would naturally appear in the order of the reading rather than separately group vocabulary, fact, and inference questions. Various types of questions should be dispersed throughout the entire selection.

It is further recommended by Marksheffel that the teacher record acceptable answers to the questions to enable him to understand the variety of correct answers students may give to each question. It is good to keep in mind that students often supply spontaneous answers which may be superior to those selected by the teacher.

The administration of a regular group informal test allows the division of students into groups of those who score 70 percent or better and those who score less than 70 percent (7). Students who score below 70 percent will have trouble reading their textbooks and may become frustrated; those who score 70 to 80 percent can read the text but will need some assistance; and those who score 80 percent or above will have no trouble reading and understanding the textbook.

SAMPLE OF GROUP INFORMAL INVENTORY

Part I   Motivation Statement

This selection is from the text, *Relationships: A Study in Human Behavior.* After you have finished reading the selection you will be asked several questions based on the reading passage. *This is not a test.* This exercise will help determine whether the text will be of use to students in this class. You will have all the time you need to complete this assignment, so relax and do your best.

Part II   Reading Selection

RIVALRY

The child's first experience with competition usually occurs within the home. Sibling rivalry—jealousy between brothers and sisters in the family—is almost a universal phenomenon. This can be observed among American families, where expression of aggression by children is more tolerated than in many other societies. Rivalry tends to be greatest when ages of children are separated by more than eighteen months but less than thirty-six months. However, spacing to avoid this critical period is not likely to make any practical difference. The jealousy of the older child focuses around his being dispossessed from a privileged place in his parents' affections. It is the older child whose reaction is likely to be most intense. Baldwin's observations showed that his reaction may be caused by the changes in the behavior of mothers toward an older child before and during pregnancy, as well as after the birth of the baby. The changes were dramatic. Over a period of a few months, the mothers showed a marked drop in affection, approval, and just plain attention, with a corresponding rise in restrictive and severe discipline.

This finding points to a major principle for dealing with sibling rivalry, or more realistically, for restricting it. It is important that the transition in the psychological status of the older child be neither too sudden nor too severe. At the same time, it is not only futile but foolhardy to try to eliminate such a change altogether, for it is a natural part of growing up.

One of the ways in which a young child tries to get over the pain of having a younger rival is to act as if he himself were no longer a child, competing on the same basis as the baby, but a third parent. Usually the left-out feeling is more apt to be experienced by the first child when the second baby arrives because the older child has been used to the spotlight and has had no practice in sharing his parents' love with others. A middle child doesn't have to decide between being a parent and being a baby when a new infant arrives. He can see that he is still just one of the children.

When a condition of intense rivalry exists, it is sometimes openly displayed, sometimes not. Rivalry is illustrated directly when a youngster tries to harm a baby brother or sister; it may be indicated indirectly when a child tries to mutilate a baby doll. Sometimes, however, children suppress feelings toward a sibling rival and even convince themselves that no rivalry exists. For example, there are adults who will say that they had no inkling of the intensity of their own bitter feelings toward a brother or sister until they reached adult years. An adult who has acknowledged only a mild rivalry situation in his childhood may, in discussing early experiences, come forth with an outburst of rage and a flood of tears.

Parental attitudes toward children's rivalries will be influenced by their own experiences.

Part III   Questions

V 1. Sibling rivalry—jealousy between brothers and sisters in a family—is almost a universal phenomenon. What does the term *sibling rivalry* mean in this sentence?

F 2. When does sibling rivalry tend to be the greatest among children?

F 3. Around what factor is the jealousy of the older child focused?

I 4. Why would sibling rivalry be considered a universal phenomenon?

F 5. What is one of the ways a young child tries to get over the pain of having a younger rival?

V 6. When a condition of intense rivalry exists, it is sometimes openly displayed, sometimes not. What does the word *intense* mean in this sentence?

I 7. Why is it important for the psychological status of a child to be changed slowly and smoothly?

F 8. Why does the middle child see that he is still just one of the children?

F 9. How are parental attitudes toward children's rivalries influenced?

I 10. Why do children suppress their feelings of rivalry?

From *Relationships: A Study in Human Behavior,* Ginn, 1972

The advantages of the group informal inventory outweigh the disadvantages. The results tell the teacher or reading specialist which students 1) can or cannot read the textbooks, 2) can or cannot answer inference questions, and 3) have vocabulary or other problems reading their textbooks. Use of the inventory also helps to identify students who need further individual testing to determine specific reading deficiencies. The reading specialist can stimulate improvement in the student's content area through successful experiences in handling reading materials on which the student later is to be graded.

According to Powell (7), the real value of the informal reading inventory is not its identification of the instructional reading level (and by interpolation, the independent and frustration levels); rather, its real value is that it affords the possibility of evaluating reading behavior in-depth. Furthermore, Powell states, the inventory represents the potential for training prospective reading teachers about reading behavior—a potential unequalled by other types of learning opportunities. For purposes of training reading teachers, the process becomes the product. Powell concludes by stating that the strength of the IRI is not as a test instrument but as a strategy for studying the behavior of the learner in a reading situation and as a basis for instant diagnosis in the teaching environment.

Administering standardized tests to students is not sufficient for diagnostic purposes. At best, these tests can be used as screening devices; and once they have served this purpose, further testing must be done to confirm or reject the results obtained on standardized tests. The reading specialist must be familiar with a variety of diagnostic techniques to build a complete picture of the student's reading habits. Informal inventories, study skills inventories, reading attitude inventories, and teacher observation must all be part of the total diagnostic process and, in some instances, visual and auditory screening may be necessary.

INFORMAL TEACHER-MADE TESTS

The reading specialist can be of immeasurable assistance to content area teachers in the community college by helping them construct informal teacher-made tests to diagnose the variety of skills students must acquire in order to function successfully in the classroom. Once teachers realize students possess differing skills and abilities, they realize the necessity for adjusting teaching techniques to accommodate individual needs of the students. Because neither standardized tests nor the Group Informal Inventory provides sufficient information about a student's readiness for learning specific content material, it is necessary for the reading specialist to show the classroom teacher how to construct informal teacher-made tests to identify students' skill weaknesses and strengths and measure their acquisition of background information or raw material.

The Entry Skills Inventory is an example of an informal teacher-made test. The following inventory was written by a reading specialist with the help of a business teacher who was about to begin a new unit on "interest" and wanted to determine whether her students could perform certain arithmetical computations, understand the subject vocabulary, and correctly spell business terms. Steps to be followed in constructing an inventory are: 1) Looking through chapters of the unit to be studied and picking out words in context which might give students problems; preparing or taking from the text, sentences containing these words and asking students to give short, written definitions of each. 2) Providing each student with a simple method for computing interest and then requiring him to solve several problems, using the method. 3) Looking through chapters to be covered and picking out words which might be difficult to spell, writing them phonetically, and asking students to rewrite them correctly.

A completed inventory which the student would answer looks like this:

PART A

Directions. The words underlined in the following sentences are taken from your textbook. From what you read in each sentence, write a short definition for each underlined word. (If you can substitute one word which you think defines or could be substituted for the underlined word, this is fine.)

1. The interest on the loan has <u>accrued</u> at the end of six months.   (accumulated)
2. The price of wheat has greatly <u>depreciated</u> now that so many farmers are growing it.   (fallen, become less)
3. Mary had to recheck all the books in order to <u>reconcile</u> the balances.   (adjust, settle)
4. Mr. Black sent a written <u>requisition</u> stating he wished to see the accounts.   (demand, request)
5. The <u>subsidiary</u> company sends its annual reports to be checked by the main company office in New York.   (auxiliary, secondary)

PART B

Directions. If a businessman borrows money, he usually is required to repay the loan plus a charge for interest. This charge will depend upon the amount borrowed (*principal*), the length of time the borrower uses the money (*time*), and the percent agreed upon (*rate*). The total payment of *maturity value* of an amount of money borrowed will be computed as follows: *principal* x *rate* x *time* = *maturity value*. Time is assumed to be one year in this case. One year is equal to 360 days. One month is equal to 30 days. To figure interest for partial years and months, follow this example: On January 12,

1972, I borrowed $300 at an interest rate of 4 percent. The maturity value is to be paid on September 16, 1972.

January has   30 days

                   -12 (day money was borrowed)

                   18 remaining days in the month of January

February-   +210 30 days x 7 months
August

September   +16 days (day to be repaid)

               244 total days on which interest will be paid

Divide this total by 30 (30 days represents a month), $244 \div 30 = 8$, with a remainder of 4. If the remainder is less than 15, these days are dropped. If the remainder is 15 or more, an extra month will be added.

Maturity value, then, is equal to principal ($300) x rate (4 percent) = $12 x time (8/12) = $8. Principal + interest — 308 (this is the maturity value).

PROBLEMS (Part B)

Solve the following interest problems using the preceding formula and directions.

1. On May 1, 1972, the Baker Company borrowed $1,000 at a rate of 6 percent. The loan plus interest is to be repaid on April 30, 1973. What will be the maturity value of the loan? ($1,060)

2. Mark borrowed $500 on April 16, 1971, at a rate of 5 percent. The loan was to be repaid with interest on December 29, 1971. What was the maturity value? ($516)

3. Rogers Publishing Company borrowed $12,000 on January 6 of this year at a rate of 6 percent. They have said that they will repay the loan with interest in exactly 10 months. What will be the day of repayment and what will be the amount they repay? (November 6, $12,600)

4. Montgomery Services loaned $15,500 to Harper Brothers at a rate of 7 percent. The loan is a 90-day loan begun on June 11, 1972. What will be the maturity value

of the note and on what day will it be repaid? (September 11, $15,771.25)

5. On May 17, 1972, Smith and Sons borrowed $9,000 from the bank at a rate of 8 percent. They will repay this loan with interest on February 12, 1973. What will be the maturity value? ($9,540)

PART C

Directions. The following words are written phonetically and you should have no difficulty in knowing what each word is. Can you *spell* each word correctly? After each printed word, write the correct spelling as best you can.

1.	ă-kowń-tunt	1. accountant
2.	ô´dit	2. audit
3.	kăn´-sĕld	3. cancelled
4.	krŏn´-o-lŏj -i-kăl	4. chronological
5.	sĭ´-fer-ing	5. ciphering
6.	kŏ- mĭsh´-ŭn	6. commission
7.	ĕg-zĕmp´-shuń	7. exemption
8.	nĕ-gō -shi-ȧ-bil´-i-ti	8. negotiability
9.	prŏ-prī´-ĕ-tēr-ship	9. proprietorship
10.	ĕk´-wi-ti	10. equity

This example of an entry skills inventory, developed by both a content area teacher and a reading specialist, demonstrates that diagnosis of skills can be incorporated into the daily classroom teaching done by the content area teacher.

Other types of informal diagnostic inventories can be developed for various content areas if the content specialist and the reading specialist act as a team to determine the goals to be achieved.

Teacher observation is another important consideration in analyzing reading problems. The reading teacher should observe student behavior in terms of lip and head movement, finger pointing, twisting, looking around, and any other behaviors which may impede effective learning. These informal observations sometimes indicate that the student cannot handle the material he is using and is probably frustrated.

The reading specialist can prepare a checklist for the content teacher and make him aware of these types of behavior activities.

When the specialist has completed the diagnosis, it is important for him to discuss with the student his reading strengths and weaknesses and plan a program for the student from the baseline established by the diagnosis. This plan should afford many successful experiences for the student so that he gains confidence in his ability and attitude toward reading and school in general.

Strang (*8*) contends that diagnosis should have a positive emphasis and be continuous and conterminous with instruction, as well as interwoven with treatment.

As a result of a study conducted to determine students' perception of their own reading problems, Artley, Burton, and Cook indicate that students are reasonably good judges of their ability and might exercise options as to the need for improving their reading ability, handling more difficult material, or engaging in more challenging tasks. Frequently, such decisions are made for students on the basis of test data only; and lacking such data, teachers feel they have no basis for guidance or suggestions. Merely asking students to assess their own ability is one way of determining their needs.

In summary, standardized tests available to the reading specialist at the community college level are limited. The tests are survey rather than diagnostic instruments and they tend to indicate the student's frustrational reading level. The IRI is a means of further testing a student's specific reading disabilities and is a strategy for studying the learner in a reading situation. It also provides a basis for instant diagnosis of reading achievement. Diagnosis is a complex and continuous process which is interwoven in the instructional sequence. The reading specialist must be aware of and familiar with as many diagnostic techniques as possible to determine a student's weaknesses and strengths and to plan a viable and successful remedial program for him. Testing should be viewed as a learning situation and the specialist should hold conferences with the students to review his strengths as well as weaknesses. Testing for testing's sake cannot serve as a learning situation for either student or teacher.

References

1. Eller, William, and Mary Attea. "Three Diagnostic Reading Tests: Some Comparisons," in J. Allen Figurel (Ed.), *Vistas in Reading*, 1966 Proceedings, Volume 11, Part 1. Newark, Delaware: International Reading Association, 1967, 562.

2. Evans, Howard M., and Eugene E. DuBois. "Community/Junior College Remedial Programs—Reflections," *Journal of Reading*, 16 (October 1972), 42.

3. Farr, Roger. *Reading: What Can Be Measured?* Newark, Delaware: International Reading Association, 1969, 121-122.

4. Goodwin, D. D. "Measurement and Evaluation of Junior College Reading Programs," *Eric/Junior College Research Reviews*, 6 (October 1971).

5. Johnson, Marjorie S., and Roy A. Kress. *Informal Reading Inventories*, Reading Aids Series. Newark, Delaware: International Reading Association, 1965.

6. Marksheffel, Ned D. *Better Reading in the Secondary School*. New York: Ronald Press, 1966, 92-94.

7. Powell, William. "The Validity of the Instructional Reading Level," in Robert E. Leibert (Ed.), *Diagnostic Viewpoints in Reading*. Newark, Delaware: International Reading Association, 1971, 121.

8. Strang, Ruth. *Reading Diagnosis and Remediation*. Newark, Delaware: International Reading Association, 1968.

9. Taschow, Horst. "The Multiple Group Silent Reading Inventory," *Reading: The Right to Participate*, National Reading Conference Yearbook, 1971.

materials and methods

Chapter Five

MATERIALS AND METHODS

MATERIALS

Since the 1950s, large numbers of hardware, software, workbooks, and kits have become available for use in the community/junior college reading center. One basic problem in selecting materials is that of determining how the materials fit into the reading program (5). The instructor is the one who must make the selection of materials for use in his own program. Some programs require both hardware and workbooks; others require combinations of many types of materials. Other programs rely heavily on one or two workbooks used independently or with accelerators to improve rate and comprehension. Some instructors use workbooks for supervised individual practice in class or for homework assignments. Materials are chosen if they contain the various types of exercises and skill drills the instructor considers to be important in his own program.

Berger and Hartig's *The Reading Materials Handbook* (1), is a useful guide for helping reading instructors to select materials. This handbook is not designed to evaluate but merely to help the teacher by providing specific descriptive information about the vast quantity of teaching and reference materials available in reading. The handbook is divided into four sections: Section One is an annotated list of texts and workbooks used as classroom teaching materials or as individualized materials, arranged alphabetically by publisher. Section Two provides an annotated list of reading tests and evaluation materials, arranged by type categories. This section also provides a list of publisher's addresses for anyone interested in obtaining further information on particular tests or pertinent test catalogs, descriptive literature, and test samples. Section Three deals with programed materials and mechanical devices for reading improvement. Section Four contains an extensive, annotated list of teacher reference works.

Ultimately, however, the choice of materials rests solely with the teacher. Criteria for using specific types of materials must include consideration of the staff who will use the materials, the objectives of the program, the student population to be served, and the cost of the materials selected.

Kits

Numerous kits are available today. Some of them are new; others have been on the market for several years. The SRA Kit IVa, written for the college level, includes rate and power builders. Both the general edition and the advanced edition of SRA's Read for Understanding are designed to develop critical reading skills at the college level.

The most recent kit to appear on the market is the McGraw-Hill Basic Skills System which includes reading, writing, spelling, vocabulary, study skills, and mathematic skills development material. The materials can be used separately or as a total program. The Basic Skills System also includes two study-type kits with reading selections that are found in most college freshman class offerings. Further information is available from McGraw-Hill, as well as a guide which gives a comprehensive overview of how the Basic Skills System materials may be used.

The ERIC/Clearinghouse for Community Colleges has published *A Directory of Self-Instructional Materials Used in Community Colleges* (2nd ed.), which lists the programed materials available in every content area in the curriculum and where these materials were developed. The reading teacher who operates a learning center will find that this publication is a valuable resource for programed and self-instructional materials, their availability and use. If possible, the teacher should visit schools listed in the Guide and see the programs in operation.

Workbooks

Over 100 workbooks are now available for use in college reading programs (a complete list of these materials appears in Appendix 2). The reading teacher should establish criteria by which he can evaluate the workbooks for use in his individual program. Many teachers have found that only certain portions of workbooks contain exercises of great value in their individual programs. Therefore, it is necessary to provide a wide variety of workbooks from which teachers may select useful portions.

Criteria should be determined by the reading staff for judging the relevance of any workbook chosen for a reading program. Suggested criteria are:

1. Do the selections have readability levels?
2. Are the answers contained within the book?
3. Does the author set purposes for the assignments and exercises in the book?
4. Is the material used in the book up-to-date and relevant to students' needs?
5. Does the book contain a variety of skill exercises or only one?
6. How long are the reading selections? Are they uniform in length or do they vary?
7. Does the workbook have removable worksheets?
8. Is there a standard pattern to the test scoring and skill exercises?
9. Is there an instructor's manual for the workbook?
10. Does the workbook instruct the students as to purposes and use of the book?
11. Are charts and graphs provided for the student to keep a record of his progress?
12. Is the workbook made of durable material? Is it soft-bound, hard bound, spiral binding?
13. Does the material in the workbook coincide with content fields?

Obviously, there are other criteria a reading staff could use in judging a workbook. Before you purchase workbook material for use in your center, ask the publisher for an examination copy of the material so you can apply your set of criteria. This saves time and money in addition to providing you with the types of materials best suited to your program. A useful suggestion for getting maximum usage from workbooks (especially on an individualized basis) is to go through each one and construct a bibliography of articles by identifying them under academic classifications such as: ASTRONOMY—Spache, p. 203; Weeden (1), pp. 117 and 122; Weeden (2), p. 90. This information tells the student he will find articles on the topic of astronomy in Spache and Berg, *The Art of Efficient Reading*, p. 203; in Weeden, *College Reader I*, pp. 117 and 122; and in Weeden, *College Reader II*, p. 90.

Material for self-use by students also may be classified by skill. For example, under the skill of *previewing*, the student will find exercises in the following material: Canavan and Heckman, *The Way to Reading Improvement*, pp. 56-81; Leedy, *A Key to Better Reading*, pp. 23-27; McDonald, *The Art of Good Reading*, pp. 27-38; Smith, *Learning to Learn*, pp. 20-22; Smith, *Faster Reading Made Easy*, pp. 90-113; Smith, *Read Faster and Get More From Your Reading*, pp. 66-85; and Spache and Berg, *The Art of Efficient Reading* (2nd ed.), pp. 3-31. The student who wants to work independently in the area of previewing has several sources of material for that purpose. This type of bibliography takes time to develop; however, it can become invaluable in individualizing instruction and allowing the student to work on his own either in skill or content areas. The reading teacher must make sure that each workbook has an answer key and a rate table so that the student can immediately check the results of his work. This arrangement can save the teacher time in grading papers and allow more time for individual conferences.

Hardware

Whenever a reading program is in the developmental stages, someone always asks: What kind of machines should I buy? How much of the budget should be spent on machines? Unfortunately, there is not a sufficient body of clear research data at this time to give an undisputed answer to these questions. More experimental investigations must be conducted under controlled conditions before we can state the exact role machines play in the teaching of reading. Research evidence tends to show that machines can be used as motivational devices for the remedial and developmental reader.

Hardware falls into several categories: 1) tachistoscope, 2) controlled reading, 3) recording, 4) skimmers and scanners, 5) accelerators, and 6) general teaching machines. Kennedy (4) points out certain dangers in using machine instruction and states that teachers who realize these dangers and plan·the remedial and developmental program with them in mind will be able to secure maximum value from the machine's capabilities and will minimize any ill effects. The greatest dangers include: 1) neglecting individual differences, 2) practicing skills in unusual situations, 3) reducing attention to individual diagnosis and planning, 4) failing to develop interest in reading per se, and 5) expecting the machine to develop the total reading program.

Caution 5 is important because many specialists plan entire reading programs around the various available machines and proceed with the mistaken belief that machines automatically create better and more interested student readers. Machinery has a definite place in a reading program when used on an individual basis to meet the skill needs of a particular student. Group use of machines has the built-in danger of being too slow for some students, causing them to lose interest, while being too fast for other students, creating complete frustration in them.

Machines have not been equally effective in all areas. Although there is disagreement in research concerning the specific machine developed skills, machines appear to be most effective for the following purposes: 1) increasing powers of discrimination, 2) developing a sight vocabulary, 3) increasing reading rate, and 4) motivating reading instruction. Needless to say, all of the previously mentioned skills can be developed without the use of machinery of any kind. Ultimately, the specialist must weigh the pros and cons for the use and purpose of machines in his program.

TEACHING METHODS

There is no one best method for teaching reading improvement. It is possible for one method to be very successful for one teacher and a complete disaster for another. Methods depend upon the teaching style of the individual instructor as well as upon the individual student receiving the instruction. The literature abounds in various program descriptions and methodology for teaching practically every reading skill. The variables of teacher, student, materials, and physical plant all must enter into the selection of teaching methods used.

Some general principles can be stated, especially for working with remedial students. Motivation is the first area with which a teacher must deal. He must help the student find personal reasons for learning. Remedial students will not be willing to devote time to learning or to practicing reading skills simply because they are assigned to a special reading class. They must have a personal desire to improve and this desire will come only if they can be convinced that reading is of value to them.

Kennedy (4) suggests that teachers prove to the student that he is capable of learning; he states that failure year after year has convinced the student of his inadequacy to learn. As soon as a specific weakness is diagnosed, it should be explained to the student and exercises or instruction should be provided to remove the obstacle. Remember, no two remedial cases are alike; what may work with one student can be a complete failure with another. Remedial programs must be individualized to fit the program with the student, not to fit the student with a particular program. The following techniques may be helpful when working with the remedial student:

1. Make reading as uncomplicated as possible. Teach only the skills that are necessary.
2. Expose the student to many kinds of reading matter. Provide books, magazines, and other reading materials that are of interest to him.
3. Begin with short assignments made in cooperation with the student.
4. Combine reading with activities that the student enjoys.
5. Use mechanical devices if the student is interested; teach the student to use them independently and provide time for him to use them for personal enjoyment.
6. Create an atmosphere of success. Spend only the time necessary on technical skills of reading. Do not burden the student with isolated drills or unessential skills.

7. Have frequent conferences with the student. Move him through a variety of skill exercises and materials.
8. Relate what the student is doing on his content work so he can see success in the area which is most important to him.

Basically, provide the student with skill exercises that will guarantee success and increase motivation (the desire to learn) and relate the skills to his content area. The teaching of transfer to the content is important to the remedial student because he needs to experience success both in the reading center and in his class work. He must see that what he is doing in the reading center has a definite relationship to what he is doing in the classroom. For example, teaching study skills such as Robinson's SQ4R provides good technique for systematized study, but unless the student uses the technique with his own texts, he sees no relationship. Teaching a student to find main ideas in a reading improvement workbook is good practice, but the student also must be taught how to do the same thing with content materials so that the skill development is not isolated from what is real and important to the student's success in school. Isolated exercises in reading improvement materials, without any transfer to what the student needs for survival, are of no value to the student unless he can see the relationship between what he does in the center and what he must do in the classroom to achieve academic success.

Vocabulary building exercises are meaningful when a student is taught to use contextual clues in his content reading. Isolated drill in vocabulary is meaningless to any student because it does not relate to his need—understanding the meaning of the text. Drill in isolated materials, followed by drill in materials the student uses every day, shows the student a relationship between the two activities and creates a desire to learn. He has a purpose for doing the exercises prescribed for improvement. Many students drop out of reading improvement programs because they cannot see any relationship between what they do in the reading center and what they do in the classroom. When a student is fighting for success and survival in the classroom, he needs assurance that his reading improvement program relates to his success in that classroom. Mere exposure to skills in the reading center does not guarantee transfer of skills to the everyday reading tasks of the student. Transfer must be taught. A purpose for learning narrows the student's field of attention and allows him to focus with greater intensity on smaller and smaller areas of the learning activity (6). New skill development should be presented in a familiar context. The teacher can build meaning by helping the student see the relationship between new ideas and previous experience. According to Seagoe, when the remedial student realizes that the quality of his work is more important than the quantity, he better understands how his work may become satisfactory even though he may produce more slowly than other students.

When planning for instruction, the teacher must remember to focus on the learning activity rather than on the teaching activity (3). The type of behavior the student exhibits determines the methods or materials used by the teacher.

We are concerned then, with two separate but related areas: the processes of instruction (teaching methods and instructional materials) and the products of instruction (knowledge, understanding, and skills).

The products of instruction depend upon the reading teacher stating a specific performance objective and describing the ways in which student behavior will be changed by interaction with the process and materials of instruction. Objectives must be expressed in terms of desired outcomes, informing the student as to what he is to do, how he is to do it, and at which level he is to perform. For example:

Identifies the main idea in paragraphs
1. Answers questions as stated in workbook with 80 percent accuracy
2. Restates the main idea in his own words with 70 percent accuracy
3. Lists the main ideas of several paragraphs with 100 percent accuracy

Each specific performance objective
1. Starts with a verb (identifies, describes, lists, relates) which directs the student to action

2. Tells the student the information to be included in the activity
3. Describes the circumstances or situation under which the student will perform
4. States the minimal acceptance criterion

What to do	How to do it	Acceptance level
Answer questions	as stated in the workbook	80 percent
Restate main ideas	in own words	70 percent
List main ideas	several paragraphs	100 percent

Specific performance objectives can require student performance at minimum or maximum levels or under prescribed time limitations.

Teachers may err by expecting too much or too little of a student and by requiring procedures under which he may be unable to perform at the set level of expectancy. Diagnosis and individual student conferences, therefore, should be interwoven in the teaching process. The teacher's job is to set realistic, individual behavioral goals for each student so that he knows what is expected of him.

Many reading centers operate on an individualized basis. Self-learning guides can be of great assistance to the reading specialist in helping to individualize the program. A self-learning guide represents any format that includes an objective and a list of materials and activities designed to help a student achieve that objective (2).

A learning guide must include the following information to make it an independent and individualized learning activity:

1. An objective stated in specific terms for the student
2. A pretest to determine the range and extent of the student's background knowledge
3. A list of materials and activities that a student may use to achieve the goals
4. A self-check built into the guide to enable the student to check his own progress
5. A posttest to check the amount of learning gained from the activity

The format used for the self-learning guides is flexible and can fit the needs of any student. It is important that the student be constantly able to check his progress. The conference allows alternate routes for the student to follow to achieve his objective.

SUMMARY

There is no one best method for the teaching of reading. The method used depends upon the teaching style of the teacher and the learning mode of the student. Basically, once the student's problem has been diagnosed, the specialist can plan his teaching approach from the level at which the student is able to perform. It is important that the student experience success and understand how his activities relate to his class work. The transfer of skills is not automatic and must be taught.

References

1. Berger and Hartig. *The Reading Materials Handbook*. New York: Academic Press, 1969.
2. Dell, Helen. *Individualizing Instruction*. Chicago: Science Research, 1972.
3. Gronlund, Norman E. *Stating Behavioral Objectives for Classroom Instruction*. New York: Macmillan, 1970.
4. Kennedy, Eddie C. *Classroom Approaches to Remedial Reading.* Itasca, Illinois: F. E. Peacock, 1971, 480, 504-505.
5. Miller, Lyle L. "Evaluation of Workbooks for College Reading Programs," *Techniques and Procedures in College and Adult Programs*, Sixth Yearbook of the Southwest Reading Conference, 1957, 75.
6. Seagoe, Mary. *The Learning Process and School Practice*. New York: Chandler, 1970, 123.

Appendix 1   PARTIAL LIST OF STANDARDIZED TESTS FOR COMMUNITY COLLEGES

Brown-Carlsen Listening Comprehension Test
Harcourt Brace Jovanovich, 1955
Grades 9-12
Forms Am, Bm
Immediate Recall
Following Directions
Recognizing Transitions
Recognizing Word Meanings
Lecture Comprehension

Buffalo Reading Test for Speed and Comprehension
Foster and Stewart
Grades 9-16
Speed, Comprehension

Cooperative English Tests: **Reading**
Cooperative Test Division: Educational Testing Service
Grades 9-14
Vocabulary, Level and Speed of Comprehension

Davis Reading Test, 1962
Psychological Corporation
Forms 1A, 1B, 1C, 1D, Series 1, Grades 11-13
Level of Comprehension
Speed of Comprehension

Diagnostic Reading Test: **Survey Action**
Science Research Associates
Upper Level, Grades 7-13
Forms A and B
Rate of Comprehension of Continuous Materials
General Vocabulary
Comprehension of Textbook Materials in Literature
Science and Social Studies

Iowa Silent Reading Test
Harcourt Brace Jovanovich, 1973
Level 1, Grades 6-9; Level 2, Grades 9-14; Level 3,
    academical accelerated high school and college
    students
Forms E & F at each level
Vocabulary
Reading Comprehension

Speed of Reading with Comprehension
Use of Reference Materials
Skimming and Scanning for Specific Information

Minnesota Speed of Reading Test for College Students
University of Minnesota Press, 1964
Forms A, B
Vocabulary
Paragraph Comprehension

Nelson-Denny Reading Test for High Schools and Colleges
Houghton-Mifflin, 1964
Forms A, B, C, D (1973)
Rate
Vocabulary
Comprehension

Peabody Library Information Test, 1940
Educational Test Bureau
College Level

The Book	Encyclopedia
Arrangement of Books	Periodicals and Indexes
Catalog	Special References
Dictionary	Bibliography

Reading Test McGraw-Hill Basic Skills System
McGraw-Hill
Forms A, B
Reading Rate and Comprehension
Skimming and Scanning
Paragraph Comprehension

Stanford Test of Academic Skills   (TASK)
Harcourt Brace Jovanovich, 1973
Level 1, Grades 8-10
Level 2, Grades 11-12, Junior/Community College
    Freshman
Separate Manual and Norms for Junior and Community
    College Freshman Reading

Stanford Diagnostic Reading Test
Harcourt Brace Jovanovich, 1973
Level III, Grades 9-13
Forms W, X
Comprehension—Literal and Inferential

Vocabulary—Word Meanings and Word Parts, Phonics,
    Phonetics, and Structural Analysis Scanning
Rate
    Skimming and Fast Reading

Study Habits Checklist
Science Research Associates
Grades 9-14

Study Skills Test McGraw-Hill Basic Skills System
McGraw-Hill
Forms A, B
Problem Solving
Underlining
Library Information
Study Skills Information
Inventory of Study Habits and Attitudes

Survey of Reading/Study Efficiency
Science Research Associates
Inventory to Diagnose Faulty Reading and Study Habits

Survey of Study Habits and Attitude
Psychological Corporation, 1967
Form C
Grades 7-12, College
Delay Avoidance
Work Methods
Study Habits
Teacher Approval
Education Acceptance
Study Attitudes

Vocabulary Test McGraw-Hill Basic Skills System
McGraw-Hill
Forms A, B
Word Knowledge
Word Parts

Watson-Glaser Critical Thinking Appraisal
Harcourt Brace Jovanovich (rev. 1964)
Forms Ym, Zm
Inference
Recognition of Assumptions
Deductions
Interpretation
Evaluation of Arguments

Appendix 2   READING IMPROVEMENT WORKBOOKS

Adams, W. Royce. *Developing Reading Versatility*
Holt, Rinehart and Winston, 1973

Adams, W. Royce. *How to Read the Humanities*
Scott, Foresman, 1969

Adams, W. Royce. *How to Read the Sciences*
Scott, Foresman, 1970

Adams, W. Royce. *Reading Through Listening*
Dickenson, 1972

Baker, William D. *Reading Skills*
Prentice-Hall, 1953

Baldridge, Kenneth P. *Reading Speed and Strategy for the Business and Professional Man*
Baldridge Reading Instruction Materials, 1966

Bamman, Hiyama, and Prescott. *World of Ideas: A Guide to Efficient Reading*
Field Educational Publications, 1970

Bamman, Hiyama, and Prescott. *Free to Read: A Guide to Efficient Reading*
Field Educational Publications, 1970

Bamman, Nordberg, and Nordberg. *World of Words: A Guide to Efficient Reading*
Field Educational Publications, 1970

Bamman, Nordberg, and Nordberg. *Free to Choose: A Guide to Efficient Reading*
Field Educational Publications, 1970

Beringause, Arthur F., and Daniel K. Lowenthal. *The Range of College Reading*
Houghton Mifflin, 1967

Bieda and Woodward. *Realizing Reading Potential*
Holt, Rinehart and Winston, 1971

Braam and Sheldon. *Developing Efficient Reading*
Oxford University Press, 1959

Brown and Adams. *How to Read the Social Sciences*
Scott, Foresman, 1968

Canavan and King. *Developing Reading Skills*
Allyn and Bacon, 1968

Canavan and Heckman. *The Way to Reading Improvement*
Allyn and Bacon, 1966

Casty, Alan. *The Act of Reading*
Prentice-Hall, 1962

Cherington, Marie R. *Improving Reading Skills in College Subjects*
Teachers College Press, 1961

Christ, Frank L. *Study Reading College Textbooks*
Science Research Associates, 1967

Cosper, Russell, and Griffin. *Towards Better Reading*
Appleton-Century-Crofts, 1967

Carter and McGinnis. *Reading: A Key to Academic Success*
William C. Brown Company, 1964

Carman and Adams. *Study Skills: A Student's Guide for Survival*
John Wiley and Sons, 1972

Dallman and Sheridan. *Better Reading in College*
Ronald Press, 1954

DeWitt, Miriam. *Reading Practical Prose*
Macmillan, 1959

Diederick, et al. *Vocabulary for College, A, B, C, D*
Harcourt, Brace and World, 1967

Edwards and Silvaroli. *Reading Improvement Program*
William C. Brown Company, 1967

Ehrlick, Murphy, and Pace. *College Developmental Reading*
The Free Press, 1968

Fisher, Joseph. *Reading to Understand Science*
McGraw-Hill, 1970

Gilbert, Doris W. *Study in Depth*
Prentice-Hall, 1966

Gilbert, Doris W. *Breaking the Reading Barrier*
Prentice-Hall, 1959

Gilbert, Doris W. *The Turning Point in Reading*
Prentice-Hall, 1969

Glock, Marvin D. *The Improvement of College Reading*
Houghton Mifflin, 1967

Gray, Lee L. *Better and Faster Reading*
Cambridge Book, 1959

Harnadek, Anita E. *Critical Reading Improvement*
McGraw-Hill, 1969

Herr, Selma. *Effective Reading for Adults* (3rd ed.)
Charles E. Merrill, 1969

Hill, Walter. *Point: A Reading System*
Wadsworth, 1970

Hill, Walter. *Basic Reading Power*
Wadsworth, 1970

Hill and Eller. *Analytical Reading*
Wadsworth, 1970

Jacobus. *Improving College Reading*
Harcourt, Brace and World, 1967

Jennings and Stevenson. *Meaning from Context: Reading for Word Study*
Allyn and Bacon, 1971

Joffee, Irwin L. *Developing Outlining Skills*
Wadsworth, 1972

Judson, Horace. *The Techniques of Reading* (3rd ed.)
Harcourt Brace Jovanovich, 1972

Kai and Kersteins. *Study-Reading for College Courses*
Macmillan, 1968

Klien, Marion H. *Dynamics of Comprehension: How to Learn from a College Textbook*
New Century Press, 1970

Krantz and Kimmelman. *Focus on Reading*
Allyn and Bacon, 1970

Leedy, Paul D. *Improve Your Reading*
McGraw-Hill, 1956

Leedy, Paul D. *A Key to Better Reading*
McGraw-Hill, 1956

Leedy, Paul D. *Read with Speed and Precision*
McGraw-Hill, 1963

Lewis, Norman. *How to Read Better and Faster*
Thomas Y. Crowell, 1944

McDonald and Simmy. *The Art of Good Reading*
Bobbs-Merrill, 1963

Maxwell, Martha. *Skimming and Scanning Improvement*
McGraw-Hill, 1969

Milan, Deanne K. *Modern College Reading*
Charles Scribner & Sons, 1971

Miller, Lyle. *Increasing Reading Efficiency* (3rd ed.)
Holt, Rinehart and Winston, 1970

Miller, Lyle. *Developing Reading Efficiency* (3rd ed.)
Burgess, 1972

Millman and Pauk. *How to Take Tests*
McGraw-Hill, 1969

Norman, Maxwell. *Successful Reading*
Holt, Rinehart and Winston, 1968

Norman, Maxwell. *How to Read and Study for Success in College*
Holt, Rinehart and Winston, 1971

Oakman, Barbara. *Countdown to Successful Reading*
Appleton-Century-Crofts, 1971

Patty and Ruhl. *The Need to Read*
Van Nostrand Reinhold, 1968

Pauk, Walter. *How to Study in College*
Houghton Mifflin, 1962

Pauk, Walter. *Reading for Success in College*
Academic Press, 1968

Raygor, Alton. *Reading for Significant Facts*
McGraw-Hill, 1969

Raygor, Alton. *Reading for the Main Idea*
McGraw-Hill, 1969

Raygor and Schick. *Reading at Efficient Rates*
McGraw-Hill, 1970

Rauch and Weinstein. *Mastering Reading Skills*
American Book, 1968

Robinson, Francis P. *Effective Reading*
Harper and Row, 1962

Sheldon and Braam. *Reading Improvement for Men and Women in Industry*
Educators Publishing Service, 1969

Slater, Lo. *Why, What, How to Read: Different Skills for Different Reading*
Random House, 1971

Spargo, Edward. *The Now Student: Freshman Reading and Study Skills*
Jamestown Publishers, 1971

Spargo, Edward (Ed.). *Selections from the Black: College Reading Skills*
Jamestown Publishers, 1970

Spargo, Giroux, and Giroux (Eds.). *Voices from the Bottom: College Reading Skills*
Jamestown Publishers, 1972

Smith, Donald E. *Learning to Learn*
Harcourt, Brace and World, 1961

Smith, Nila B. *Faster Reading Made Easy*
Popular Library, 1963

Smith, Nila B. *Read Faster and Get More from Your Reading*
Prentice-Hall, 1957

Spache and Berg. *The Art of Efficient Reading* (2nd ed.)
Macmillan, 1966

Strang, Ruth. *Study Type Reading Exercises*
Teachers College Press, 1951

Stroud, Ammons, and Bamman. *Improving Reading Ability*
Appleton-Century-Crofts, 1949

Van Zandt, Eleanor (Ed.). *Pattern for Reading*
Scholastic Magazines, 1970

Wainwright, Gordon. *Towards Efficiency in Reading*
Cambridge University Press, 1968

Appendix 3   PROFESSIONAL ORGANIZATIONS

International Reading Association
800 Barksdale Road
Newark, Delaware 19711

National Reading Conference
Appalachian State University
Boone, North Carolina 28607

Western College Reading Association
Box 23113
Pleasant Hills, California 94528

The College Reading Association
Leonard Braam
Reading and Language Arts Center
Syracuse University
Syracuse, New York 13210

North Central Reading Association
David M. Wark
University of Minnesota
Minneapolis, Minnesota 55455

IRA/SIG Two Year Colleges
Judith Mayer
113 Irwin Street
Springfield, New Jersey 07081

Eric Clearinghouse For Junior Colleges
96 Powell Library Building
University of California
Los Angeles, California 90024

American Education Research Association
Special Interest Group, Community Junior College
     Research
Eric Clearinghouse for Junior Colleges
96 Powell Library Building
University of California
Los Angeles, California 90024